A FATHER
A HERO

PRESENTED TO

FROM

DATE

This book is dedicated with appreciation and respect to fathers everywhere who are doing their best to raise their children in the fear and admonition of the Lord. May God grant you increasing measures of strength and wisdom as you embrace that awesome responsibility.

James Dobson

First let me say it is an honor to do this with Dr. James Dobson, a man who has done so much to help families in trouble and to teach godly principles that help save families from the false values thrown at us by the world. He is a dear friend and godly man.

Living in a time and a country where the family is so shattered and in disarray, I am privileged to be able to use my art in any way that might help people realize the importance of the father in the family structure. The need for the father to be a living example of Christ's love for his wife and children and live an honorable life before God and his fellow man is the most important job we've been given. Fellas, let's do it right.

G. Harvey

A FATHER
A HERO

Inspiration and Insights for Every Dad

By DR. JAMES DOBSON
Paintings by G. HARVEY

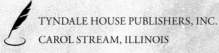
TYNDALE HOUSE PUBLISHERS, INC.
CAROL STREAM, ILLINOIS

Visit Tyndale's exciting Web site at www.tyndale.com

TYNDALE and Tyndale's quill logo are registered trademarks of Tyndale House Publishers, Inc.

A Father, A Hero

Copyright © 2005 by James Dobson, Inc. All rights reserved.

First printing by Tyndale House Publishers, Inc., in 2007.

Artwork by G. Harvey. All artwork contributed for *A Father, A Hero* is an original creation of G. Harvey's and ownership of all images reproduced from *A Father, A Hero* are the exclusive property of and copyrighted to and in the name of G. Harvey, LTD and G. Harvey, Inc.

Cover and interior design by Koechel Peterson & Assoc., Inc., Minneapolis, Minnesota

Previously published by Multnomah Publishers, Inc., under ISBN 1-59052-497-7. *Multnomah* is a trademark of Multnomah Publishers, Inc., and is registered in the U.S. Patent and Trademark Office.

Unless otherwise indicated, all Scripture quotations are taken from the *Holy Bible*, New International Version®. NIV®. Copyright © 1973, 1978, 1984 by International Bible Society. Used by permission of Zondervan. All rights reserved.

Tyndale House Publishers, Inc., has made every effort to provide proper and accurate source attribution for all selections used in this book. Should any attribution be found to be incorrect, the publisher welcomes written documentation supporting correction for subsequent printings. We gratefully acknowledge the cooperation of other publishers and individuals who have granted permission for use of their material.

ISBN-13: 978-1-4143-1743-4

ISBN-10: 1-4143-1743-3

Printed in Singapore

13 12 11 10 09 08 07
 7   6   5   4   3   2   1

He *dreams*, he plans,
he struggles that *we* might
have the *best*. His sacrifice is
quiet, his *life* is love expressed.

AUTHOR UNKNOWN

Table of Contents

A FATHER, A PROVIDER

A FATHER, A SPIRITUAL ROLE MODEL

Every child needs a hero.

When I was young, it was common practice to study those who had led exemplary lives—courageous men and women who succeeded against all odds. Our heroes were leaders and role models such as Abraham Lincoln, Winston Churchill, and Florence Nightingale. They inspired us to reach for the best within us.

Today, thanks in part to our society's fascination with human failure, that tradition has fallen by the wayside. There is less emphasis on past achievers, while contemporary sports stars, entertainers, and political figures, with all their flaws on display, just don't measure up. From watching the news or reading the papers, one would think that boys and girls living in the twenty-first century would find *no one* worthy of their respect and admiration.

Yet there is one person—one man—that every child longs to look up to, to emulate, to know that he or she can count on when the chips are down. He is the one that all children, in the deep reaches of their hearts, want most as a hero.

Dad.

For thousands of years in nations and cultures around the world, it has been fathers whom families turned to in times of crisis, men who assumed the mantle of leadership when others would not or could not step forward, who have set the moral and spiritual example for their wives and children, and who have quietly served, in so many ways, as the backbone of their societies. Until recently, the phrase "a good family man" was seen as more than a cliché or an idea to be ridiculed by postmodernists and the media. It represented self-sacrifice, honesty, kindness, dedication, and industry. Not every dad achieved this standard of excellence, of course, but it was what we, his family and friends, expected and needed him to be.

There is still a great need for strength and confidence in the midst of the inevitable storms of life, and that role falls more naturally to men. As a huge oak tree provides shelter and protection for all the living things that nest in its branches, a strong man provides security and comfort for every member of his family. He knows who he is as a child of God and what is best for his wife and children. He would give his life for his family if they were threatened. His sons and daughters, especially, want and need the protection and guidance of just such a man.

A father. A hero.

Despite what may seem like a dearth of heroes in our world today, outstanding men of character still exist in enormous numbers. More than four hundred police officers and firefighters, many of them husbands and fathers, sacrificed their lives trying to rescue office workers from New York's Twin Towers on September 11, 2001. These men, and the women who worked beside them, are heroes.

On that same fateful day, Todd Beamer, a father of two little boys with a daughter on the way, uttered the battle cry "Let's roll!" on Flight 93 and helped prevent a deliberate crash into the White House or the Capitol building. Todd and the others who died with him on that day are heroes.

The title of "hero" is not defined only by bravery and life-giving sacrifice, however. Most fathers give their lives in a more subtle way, through the many choices they make for the benefit of their families. Though these dads are rarely recognized for their dedication and sacrifice, their steady commitment to traditional faith and values is the foundation of every new generation. Every one of them deserves the title "good family man," and most of them could be considered heroes.

My own father, Rev. James Dobson Sr., was such a man. He exemplified what I believe to be God's concept of a husband and father. Most of my writings are an expression of his views and teachings. He was a man who deeply loved the Lord and his wife of forty-two years. I have also known, from the earliest moments of awareness, that he loved me.

The happiest days of my life occurred when I was between ten and thirteen years of age. My dad and I would arise very early before the sun came up on a wintry morning. We would put on our hunting clothes and heavy boots, and drive twenty miles from the little town where we lived. After parking the car, we climbed over a fence and entered a wooded area which I called the "big woods," because the trees seemed so large to me. We would slip down to the creek bed and follow that winding stream several miles back into the forest.

Then my dad would hide me under a fallen tree that made a little room with its branches. He would find a similar shelter for himself around a bend in the creek. There we would await the arrival of the sun and the awakening of the animal world. Little squirrels and birds and chipmunks would scurry back and forth, not knowing they were being observed. My dad and I watched as the breathtaking panorama of the morning unfolded, which spoke so eloquently of the God who made all things.

But most importantly, there was something dramatic that occurred between my dad and me on those mornings. An intense love and affection was generated that set the tone for a lifetime of fellowship. There was a closeness and a oneness that made me want to be like that man…that made me choose his values as my values, his dreams as my dreams, his God as my God.

If any human being that I have known deserved the title of "hero," it was my dad.

This book is, in part, a call to fathers everywhere to return to the traditional and biblical values portrayed by men such as Todd Beamer and James Dobson Sr. It is encouragement for men to become the kind of dad their families need:

Fathers who are leaders according to the responsibilities and limits spelled out in Scripture.

Fathers who are protectors, shielding their families from the dangers of the outside world and teaching them how to cope with them successfully.

Fathers who are providers, capable and willing to assume the role of breadwinner in order to assure the financial security of their families.

Fathers who are spiritual role models, offering the direction and example that will guide each of their loved ones to a meaningful and lasting faith.

Some may consider these duties old-fashioned, but there is timeless wisdom to be found here. Men have been defined by these responsibilities for millennia, and for good reason. It is the stuff of heroes.

This book aspires to another,

equally important purpose—to celebrate fatherhood and fathers everywhere. The encouraging stories you will find here describe dads from many walks of life—sometimes struggling, sometimes succeeding, and always doing their best. The book is illustrated with paintings by my dear friend, the gifted artist Gerald Harvey. If you are a man and a father, I hope his works will help inspire you to be the best role model and leader you can be.

Such inspiration is needed, because your role as dad is incredibly challenging. I know—I've been there! There are times when you wonder if you are achieving your goals, and other moments when you feel like throwing in the towel. That is especially true for those in the "sandwich generation," who are increasingly responsible for their aging parents *and* their rambunctious teens. The financial pressures and the personal demands may seem overwhelming at times. Yet if you stay the course, you will secure not only the best for those you love, but also that of generations to come. Nothing could be more important or, ultimately, more rewarding.

Therefore, Dad, for your unswerving commitment to your family—for making the right choices regardless of personal loss or sacrifice—for leading, protecting, and providing—for encouraging your family to love Jesus Christ and follow the wisdom of Scripture—I say on behalf of sons and daughters everywhere, "Thank you."

Every child needs a hero.

You are that man!

A FATHER, A LEADER

"He tends his *flock*
like a shepherd…
he *gently* leads
those that have *young.*"

ISAIAH 40:11

STANDING TALL

STEVE FARRAR

HEN I WAS A SOPHOMORE in high school, we moved to a new town and a new high school. It was the typical scenario of being the new kid who doesn't know anyone. One of the fastest ways to make friends in a situation like that is to go out for a sport. In about two days you know more guys from playing ball than you could meet in three months of going to school.

Normally, I would have gone out for basketball. But I had done something very foolish. I had brought home a D on my last report card. The only reason I had gotten a D was that I had horsed around in the class and basically exhibited some very irresponsible behavior in turning in papers. My dad had a rule for the three boys in our family: If any of us got anything lower than a C in a class, we couldn't play ball. He didn't demand that we get straight A's or make the honor roll. But my dad knew that the only reason any of us would get a D was that we were fooling around instead of being responsible.

As a result, I didn't go out for basketball. Now, my dad was all for me playing ball. He had been all-state in both basketball and football in high school, went to college on a basketball scholarship, and after World War II was offered a contract to play football for the Pittsburgh Steelers. He wanted me to play. But he was more interested in developing my character than he was in developing my jump shot.

One day in my physical education class we were playing basketball. I didn't know it, but the varsity coach was in the bleachers watching the pickup game. After we went into the locker room, he came up to me and asked me who I was and why I wasn't out for varsity basketball. I told him that we had just recently moved into town and that I'd come out for basketball next year. He said that he wanted me to come out this year.

I told him that my dad had a rule about getting any grade lower than a C.

The coach said, "But according to the school rules, you're still eligible to play if you have just one D."

"Yes, sir, I realize that," I replied. "But you have to understand that my dad has his own eligibility rules."

"What's your phone number?" the coach asked. "I'm going to call your dad."

"I'll be happy to give you the phone number, but it will be a waste of your time," I said.

This coach was a big, aggressive guy. He was about six feet two inches and 220 pounds, which put him one inch shorter and twenty pounds lighter than my dad. Coach was used to getting his way. But he hadn't met my dad. I knew before the coach ever called what my dad's answer would be.

Was my dad capable of change?

Sure he was. Was he going to change because he got a call from the varsity coach? Of course not. That night after dinner, Dad told me the coach had called. He told me he had told the coach no. He then reminded me of the importance of being responsible in class and that he really wanted me to play basketball. But the ball was in my court (no pun intended). If I wanted to

play it was up to me. At that point, I was very motivated to work hard in class so that I could play basketball the next season.

The next morning the coach came up to me in the locker room. "I talked to your dad yesterday afternoon and he wouldn't budge. I explained the school eligibility rules, but he wouldn't change his mind. I don't have very much respect for your father."

I couldn't believe my ears. This coach didn't respect my father. Even I had enough sense to know that my dad was doing the right thing. Sure, I wanted to play ball, but I knew that my dad was a man of his word and he was right in not letting me play. I couldn't believe this coach would say such a thing.

"Coach," I said. "I can tell you that I highly respect my dad. And I also want you to know that I will never play basketball for you."

I never did. I got my grades up, but I never went out for varsity basketball. I refused to play for a man who didn't respect my dad for doing what was right. That was the end of my high school basketball career because that man coached basketball for my remaining years in high school.

Come to think of it, the real reason I wouldn't join his team was that I didn't respect him. He was a compromiser, and I suspected that he would do anything to win. My dad was a man of conviction and a man of character. And any coach who couldn't see that was not the kind of man I wanted to associate with. My dad was strict and unwilling to change his conviction even though it hurt him for me not to play ball. My dad was capable of change, but he was unwilling to change because he had a long-term objective for my life that the coach didn't have.

The coach wanted to win games. My dad wanted to build a son.

HEAD OF THE HOUSE

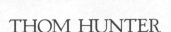

THOM HUNTER

MY PRETEEN SON PATRICK doesn't take many things seriously, but occasionally something grabs hold of him and he just won't let it go. He will question an idea or concept until he is satisfied that society isn't misleading him and that all is right in his world.

I'm never prepared for his persistence.

"Dad, can we go to the movies today?" he asked as we crawled down the optimistically named Northwest Expressway.

"Maybe," I said. "I'll check with Mom when we get home."

"She'll say no," he said. "She'll say we need to clean our rooms, or read a book, or play outside. Or…or something else."

The tires on the van made a couple more rotations.

"Dad?" asked Patrick. "Can we get another hamster?"

What a radical idea. We hadn't had a hamster die on us in weeks.

"Well, maybe," I answered. "We'll see what Mom thinks."

I turned off the radio.

"Dad?" came the voice again. "Can we eat out tonight?"

"Probably," I said. "If Mom doesn't already have something planned."

I pushed a cassette tape into the player.

"Dad?" Patrick asked. "Is Mom the head of our house?"

Wham! I felt like I was in a ten-car pileup. My face was turning red. My temperature was rising. I was suddenly feeling closed in by the cars surrounding me. I looked in the rearview mirror. Patrick was perched in the middle of the seat behind me, an innocent little grin on his face.

"Patrick," I said, "I am the head of the household. I make the decisions. And don't you forget it. Understand?"

"Okay," he said. "Does that mean we can eat out, go to the movies, and pick up a new hamster on the way home?"

He'd set me up. And I almost fell for it. He was watering down the parent partnership, looking for a crack in which to stick a wedge, testing a biblical concept, and looking for the advantage in the process.

What do pizza, hamsters, and big-screen fantasy have to do with whether or not I am fulfilling my role as head of the family? I asked myself that question as I zeroed in on the bumper in front of me. I slammed on the brakes and avoided the accident. Fortunately, we were at the expressway's top speed of seven miles an hour.

For scoring purposes, we did eat out and go to the movies that night, but we decided to sell the hamster cage. "We" made those decisions, his mother and I.

This "head of the household" thing is very touchy to me. When I was growing up, there was never any doubt. Mother was the head of the household. But she had never intended it to be that way. She was supposed to have had a partner. She understood the concept of a helpmeet. If my father had been a different kind of man and hadn't left us when I was six years old, she would have made a wonderful complement to him.

"You must be a man," she would tell me when I was a teenager. "Take the responsibility; don't run from the decisions; love your wife; cherish your children."

And be the head of the household.

So I always wanted to be the head of the household: ruler over all I surveyed, supreme commander, father and master of my many loyal subjects. I carried this dream to the altar and later into the delivery room—five times. My kingdom went from squalling to crawling to sprawling all around me.

So, if I am the head of the household, why is the head aching and the house barely holding together? And if I am the head of the household, why do I sometimes go to bed with dishpan hands and worry that I've forgotten to unplug the iron?

If I am the head of the household, why do I have to barter for time to watch a football game on television, promising to ride bikes for two hours in exchange for ten minutes of solitude?

And, if I am the head of the household, why do I have to cut my subjects' plates of meat after I set the table? And why do I have to clear the table and pick up mushy mashed potatoes from the floor with my bare hands while everyone else has dessert they weren't supposed to get unless they ate all their mashed potatoes?

And, if I am the head of the household, why do I have to cover five other

bodies before I pull my own blanket up to my own chin; explain away everybody else's nightmares before I take on my own; fluff their pillows and tuck their feet back under the sheets; get them one more drink; and plug in their night-lights?

And if I am the head of the household, why do I have to rub my wife's back before she can go to sleep?

Why, I ask? Why do I have to do all these things? Because I am the head of the household, that's why. If I don't listen…if I am inconsiderate of others…if I make decisions without the input of the wife God gave me…if I try to do it on my own without God, then I may as well forget about being the head of the household.

That's what I'll tell Patrick next trip down the Northwest Expressway. We'll have plenty of time.

*I*t's not easy to be head of the household these days, is it? It seems that wherever we turn, the role of a man as leader of his family is being questioned and undermined—by the media, by feminists, by certain high school basketball coaches looking to cut corners, and sometimes, as Thom Hunter learned in the previous story, even by our own children!

It has not always been so. Throughout human history, fathers have served as the leaders of their clans. In their homes, they were the final arbiters on issues of substance. Only in recent decades has that position been challenged.

Today, the controversy over masculine leadership at home has caused considerable confusion in the minds of many fathers. Fortunately, the Lord has given us biblical truths to clear away the fog.

It all begins with the instruction of the apostle Paul: "Husbands, love your wives, just as Christ loved the church and gave himself up for her to make her holy…. In this same way, husbands ought to love their wives as their own bodies" (Ephesians 5:25–28). Paul also tells us "the husband is the head of the wife as Christ is the head of the church" (Ephesians 5:23).

In other words, we men are charged with the holy, loving leadership of our wives. There is nothing dictatorial or selfish in this prescription! Our love is to be so strong that it mirrors Christ's love for the church, so committed that we would unquestioningly die to save her, and so powerful that it is indistinguishable from love of self.

That love applies just as much to the leading of our children. Scripture again provides the blueprint: A father should encourage and comfort his sons and daughters, urging them to "live lives worthy of God" (1 Thessalonians 2:11–12). He is charged with instruction (Proverbs 1:8–9) and discipline (Hebrews 12:10) of his offspring. A father must not "exasperate" his children as he does these things. Instead—and most important of all—he is to "bring them up in the training and instruction of the Lord" (Ephesians 6:4).

In the face of these enormous responsibilities, you may feel like a high school dropout interviewing for a job as a nuclear physicist—you know that your resume doesn't measure up. But be encouraged! Scripture tells us that our heavenly Father will assist us in each of life's heavy responsibilities: "The LORD will guide you always; he will satisfy your needs" (Isaiah 58:11).

Leadership means not only discerning the right course of action, but also following through with it even when it is difficult or painful to do so. Steve Farrar's father, a Christian who relied on the Lord's direction to lead his family, understood this. His firm convictions about the lessons he was teaching his son were rooted in the authority of God's Word. My father (and mother) also depended on the Lord's wisdom in raising me, and Shirley and I attempted to do the same while bringing up our children. You too can rely on almighty God, the Father of all fathers, for strength and guidance as you lead your family. No matter what your qualifications or what others may say, you are the right man for the job.

James Dobson

A FATHER, A PROTECTOR

"When a *strong* man,
fully *armed*,
guards his own house,
his possessions are *safe*."

LUKE 11:21

JUST WAITIN' FOR YOU

STU WEBER

SOME YEARS AGO while speaking at a parenting conference with Dennis Rainey, I heard Dennis tell a story which moved my masculine heart to intense emotion and determination. Maybe it will encourage you, too.

In the mid-1980s a missionary family serving overseas came home on furlough, needing a little R & R. Through the graciousness of friends, they'd been provided with the use of a summer home on a beautiful lake. For these tired, frontline warriors, it was like a little piece of Eden.

One bright summer morning, Mom was in the kitchen fussing with the baby and preparing a lunch for the family. Dad was in the boathouse puttering with something that needed some puttering. And the three children present were out on the lawn between the home and the edge of the lake. Three-year-old "little Billy" was under the care of a five-year-old sister and a twelve-year-old cousin.

When Sister and Cousin became distracted with some mutual interest, little Billy decided it would be an opportune time to wander down to the water and check out that shiny little aluminum boat that had been bobbing so temptingly beside the dock. The trouble is, three-year-olds have limited experience in getting from a stable dock to a bobbing boat. With one foot on the dock and the other stretching toward the boat, Billy lost his balance and fell into five or six feet of water beside the dock.

The splash alerted the twelve-year-old, who let loose a piercing scream.

That brought Dad on the run. After scoping out the situation for a second or two, he dove into the murky water and began a desperate search for his little boy. But the lake water was murky, and Dad couldn't see a thing. With lungs desperate for air, he resurfaced, grabbed another ragged gasp, and plunged back under. Sick with panic, the only thing he could think to do was to extend his arms and legs as far as he could and try to *feel* little Billy's whereabouts. Having nearly exhausted his oxygen supply a second time, he began to ascend once again for another breath.

On his way up, he felt little Billy, arms locked in a death grip to a pier post some four feet under water. Prying the boy's fingers loose, they burst together through the surface to fill their lungs with life-giving air.

Adrenaline continued to surge. Conversation would not return to normal for a long time. Dad just carried little Billy around, holding him close, unable to put him down. Finally, when heart rates and nerves had calmed a bit, this missionary dad turned to his boy with a question.

"Billy, what on earth were you *doing* down there, hanging onto that post so far underwater?"

Little Billy's reply, laced with all the wisdom of a tot, reaches out and grabs us all by the throat.

"Just waitin' for you, Dad. Just waitin' for you!"

Billy was saying, in the language of a three-year-old, "Dad, I knew you'd come. I knew you'd be there for me. I knew you'd save me. I knew you wouldn't leave me. You're a man. You're my king.

"You're my dad."

OF MORE VALUE

JERRY B. JENKINS

FRIEND, THE FATHER of two daughters, admits he doesn't mind putting a little fear into the boys. His daughters may be embarrassed when he asks for a few moments alone with their dates, and he might rather the young men think he's an okay guy than that he's a mean, protective father. But some things are worth a little awkwardness. Boys might think such dads are a little overprotective. To the fathers of daughters, however, there is no such thing as overprotective.

Another friend says he uses a sports car analogy to get his point across. He'll say to the boy, "If I owned the most

expensive, exotic sports car on the road and I let you take it for a spin, you'd be careful with it, wouldn't you?"

"Oh, yes sir, you bet."

"You'd treat it better than if it were your own, wouldn't you?"

"Yes, sir."

"I wouldn't want to think you were screeching the tires, would I?"

"No, sir."

"Well, let me tell you something, just so we're straight with each other, man to man. My daughter is of infinitely more value to me than any car could be. Do you get my drift? She's on loan from me to you for the next few hours, and I wouldn't want to discover that she was treated with any less care or respect than I would give her. I'm responsible for her. She's mine. I'm entrusting her to you. That trust brooks no second chances. Understand?"

By then, of course, the young man is wondering why he didn't ask someone else out. He's only nodding, unable to speak. Most often, he brings the girl home earlier than promised. The daughter might even complain about her father's approach, but deep down she feels loved and cherished, and you can be sure she'll marry a man who treats her that way.

MANHOOD AT ITS BEST

DR. JAMES DOBSON

HOW CAN WE GET a handle on the ephemeral qualities of character and strength in a man of God? It is understood most readily by observing a good *model*, and I crossed paths momentarily with one of the finest a few years ago.

My family had joined me at Mammoth, California, for a weekend ski outing. The kids were still young, and I was working frantically to teach them the fundamentals of the sport. That's a tough assignment, as every skiing father knows. You can guess who gets to carry *all* the skis, boots, and poles, and then park the car, stand in line to buy the lift tickets, herd the clan toward the ski slopes, and get everyone zipped up and ready to go. At that precise moment, inevitably, one of the children announces that he or she has to go to the bathroom. Upon hearing that important news, Dad clomps back down the hill with his child in tow, and then goes through the zippety-zip process twice more. Then he trudges back up the mountain. That is how the system works on a *good* day.

On a bad morning, some of the most frustrating experiences in life can occur. Children are fully capable of announcing this need to visit the john one at a time, sending Dad up and

down the mountain like a yo-yo. By the time he and the last child get back, the first one has to go again. Kids seem to delight in losing valuable equipment, too, such as leather gloves, designer wool hats, ski jackets, etc. They're also good at bickering, which drives their harried parents crazy.

On the particular day in question, it was a *bad* morning for my family. Our children did everything wrong. There we were on a family vacation to produce a little togetherness, but I couldn't stand either one of my kids. They complained and dawdled and spread clothes all over the city of Mammoth. Maybe it will make other families feel better to know that the Dobsons have nerve-wracking days like that. By the time I transported the family to the ski lodge, I was well on my way to total irritation. Danae and Ryan climbed out of the car with a grumble, and I headed toward a parking lot a mile or so away. On the way down the hill I muttered a brief prayer. Actually, it was more of an expression of exasperation than anything else.

"What am I going to do with these kids you've given to me?" I said to the Lord, as though it were His fault. He did not reply.

I parked the car and walked back to an assembly area where a flatbed truck comes by every ten minutes to pick up passengers. About fifteen skiers stood awaiting a ride up the mountain, and I quietly joined them. Then I noticed a "different" young lady standing with the others. She turned to look at me, and I observed the unmistakable appearance of mental retardation in her eyes. This late teenager was behaving in a very strange way. She stood facing the mountain, quoting the word "whomever" over and over. "Whomever!" she said in a loud voice. A few seconds later, she repeated the word nonsensically.

Having worked with developmentally disabled individuals for years, I felt an instant empathy for this girl. It was apparent, however, that the other skiers didn't share my concern. They were young, attractive, and beautifully outfitted. I watched them glance in the direction of the girl and then take a step or two backward. They rolled their eyes at each other as if to say, "Who's the 'crazy' we have with us?"

About that time the truck arrived, and all of us began climbing aboard. As the driver took us toward the ski lodge, the retarded girl continued to face the mountain and say the word "whomever." By this time she stood alone, as the "in crowd" left her isolated at the center of the truck bed. She was alone, that is except for a big man who stood nearby. Suddenly, I realized that he was her father.

It was at that point that this man with the kind face did something I will never forget. He walked over to his daughter and wrapped his arms around her. He put his big hand on the back of her head and gently pressed it to his chest. Then he looked down at her lovingly and said, "Yeah, babe. Whomever."

I must admit that I had to turn my head to conceal the moisture in my eyes. You see, that father had seen the same rejection from the beautiful people that I had observed. He saw their smiles…their scorn. His act of love to the girl was only partially done for her benefit. The father was actually speaking to all of us.

He was saying, "Yes, it's true. My daughter is retarded. We can't hide that fact. She is very limited in ability. She won't sing the songs. She won't write the books. In fact, she's already out of school. We've done the best we could for her. But I want you all to know something. This young lady is my girl, and I love her. She's the whole world to me. And I'm not ashamed to be identified with her. 'Yeah, babe. Whomever!'"

The selfless love and tenderness of that father flooded out from his soul and engulfed mine. Instantly, I felt compassion and love for our two children.

"All right, Lord!" I said. "I get the message."

Two weeks later, I was a guest on a national television show, and the moderator gave me four and a half minutes to answer such questions as "How did the institution of the family get into such a mess, and how can we correct the problem?"

I couldn't have answered that question in four and a half *hours*…but I can say this: One of the solutions to family disintegration has something to do with what that father was feeling for his handicapped girl, there in the back of that flatbed truck at a ski lodge in Mammoth, California.

*W*e dads bear a heavy responsibility when it comes to protecting our children. Sometimes that duty goes well beyond reminding our kids to look both ways before crossing the street, as the father of little Billy discovered while desperately trying to rescue his son at the lake. It was a harrowing experience for the father, but far less so for his son. Billy never doubted that his dad would come through. That's simply the kind of trust kids place in their fathers. Most of us wouldn't have it any other way.

There are times, though, when we fathers are called on to protect our children in ways they simply cannot understand. I remember such an incident from my son's early childhood. Ryan had a terrible ear infection when he was three years old that kept him (and his parents) awake most of the night. Shirley bundled up the toddler the next morning and took him to see the pediatrician. This doctor was an older man with very little patience for squirming kids. He wasn't overly fond of parents, either.

After examining Ryan, the doctor told Shirley that the infection had adhered itself to the eardrum and could only be treated by pulling the scab loose with a wicked little instrument. He warned that the procedure would hurt, and instructed Shirley to hold her son tightly on the table. Not only did this news alarm her, but enough of it was understood by Ryan to send him into orbit. It didn't take much to do that in those days.

Shirley did the best she could. She put Ryan on the examining table and attempted to hold him down. But he would have none of it. When the doctor inserted the pick-like instrument in his ear, the child broke loose and screamed to high heaven. The pediatrician then became angry with Shirley and told her if she couldn't follow instructions she'd have to go get her husband. I was in the neighborhood and quickly came to the examining room. After hearing what was needed, I swallowed hard and wrapped my two-hundred-pound, six-foot-two-inch frame around the toddler. It was one of the toughest moments in my career as a parent.

What made it so emotional was the horizontal mirror that Ryan was facing on the back side of the examining table. This made it possible for him to look directly at me as he screamed for mercy. I really believe I was in greater agony in that moment than my terrified little boy. It was too much. I turned him loose—and got a beefed-up version of the same bawling out that Shirley had received a few minutes earlier. Finally, however, the grouchy pediatrician and I finished the task.

I reflected later on what I was feeling when Ryan was going through so much suffering. What hurt me was the look on his face. Though he was screaming and couldn't speak, he was "talking" to me with those big blue eyes. He was saying, "Daddy! Why are you doing this to me? I thought you loved me. I never thought you would do anything like this! How could you…? Please, please! Stop hurting me!"

It was impossible to explain to Ryan that his suffering was necessary for his own good, that I was trying to help him, that it was love that required me to hold him on the table. How could I tell him of my compassion in that moment? I would gladly have taken his place on the table, if possible. I would go through such an experience a thousand times for the sake of my kids. It is simply what a "protector" must do.

The role of protector, however, goes even further, as the tender-hearted father and his retarded daughter demonstrated on the way to the ski slopes years ago. He understood that the security a dad provides is not only against physical dangers—burglars, bullies, and the like—

but also against ridicule, self-doubt, and even cultural threats such as pornography and warped messages that undermine cherished family values. He stood ready to protect every aspect of his disadvantaged daughter—her body, her mind, and her spirit.

This is what fatherhood—in fact masculinity itself—is all about. It embodies the time-honored qualities of men that have been marginalized and misunderstood in recent decades in this country. This is a type of manliness that Wall Street Journal columnist Peggy Noonan, writing in the aftermath of the 2001 terrorist attacks, says may be coming back.

"I am speaking of masculine men," Noonan wrote, "men who push things and pull things and haul things and build things, men who charge up stairs in a hundred pounds of gear and tell everyone else where to go to be safe. Men who are welders, who do construction, men who are cops and firemen. They are all of them, one way or another, the men who put the fire out, the men who are digging the rubble out, and the men who will build whatever takes its place.

"And their style is back. We are experiencing a new respect for *their old-fashioned masculinity, a new respect for physical courage, for strength and for the willingness to use both for the good of others."*

I pray that Peggy Noonan is right, that masculinity is making a comeback. Because we need such men. And families need such fathers.

It is the father who understands and adopts this kind of masculinity who will do all he can to protect his family. His very presence at home is a welcome comfort. It offers safety and security. It holds out the promise of wise counsel. It extends unconditional love.

And when the day is done and wife, sons, and daughters are all tucked into bed, each member of this father's family will sleep a little more soundly knowing that Dad is there.

James Dobson

A FATHER, A PROVIDER

"A *righteous* man...
gives his *food*
to the hungry
and *provides* clothing
for the naked."

EZEKIEL 18:5–7

A SECRET PROMISE KEPT

BRIAN KEEFE

EVERY TIME I PASS a fire station, the red fire engines with shining chrome, the smell of drying hoses and freshly polished floors, the oversized rubber boots and helmets, all transport me back to my childhood, to the firehouse where my father worked for thirty-five years as head of maintenance.

One day, my dad let me and my older brother Jay slide down the sparkling gold fire pole. In the corner of the station was the "creeper" used to slide under trucks when men were repairing them. Dad would say "Hold on" and spin me until I was dizzy. It was better than any Tilt-a-Whirl ride.

Next to the creeper was an old soda machine that dispensed the original, green, ten-ounce bottles of Coca-Cola for ten cents. A trip to the soda machine was always the highlight of our visit.

When I was ten years old, I took two of my friends by the station to show my dad off. I asked Dad if we could each have a soda before we went home for lunch.

I detected just the slightest hesitation in my father's voice. But he said "sure" and gave us each a dime. We raced to the soda machine to see whose bottle cap might hold the illustrious star on the inside.

What a lucky day! My cap had a star. I was only two caps away from sending for my very own Davy Crockett hat.

We all thanked my father and headed home for lunch and a summer afternoon of swimming.

When I came home from the lake, I heard my parents talking. Mom seemed upset with Dad, and then I heard my name mentioned: "You should have just said you didn't have money for sodas. Brian would have understood. We don't have any extra money, and you need to have your lunch."

My dad, in his usual way, just shrugged it off.

Before I could be caught listening, I hurried upstairs to the room I shared with my four brothers.

As I emptied my pockets, ready to put my new bottle cap with the other seven, I suddenly realized how great a sacrifice my father had made for it. That night I made a promise: Someday I'd tell my father that I knew of the sac-rifice he made that afternoon and on so many other days, and I'd never forget him for it.

Over the next twenty years, my father's lifestyle—working three jobs to support the nine of us—caught up to him. He suffered four heart attacks, finally ending up with a pacemaker.

One afternoon Dad's old blue sta-tion wagon was broken down, and he asked me to take him to his doctor's appointment. As I pulled up to the firehouse, I saw Dad outside with the other firemen, crowded around a brand-new pickup truck. It was a beauty. When I admired it, Dad said,

"Someday, I'll own a truck like that."

We both laughed. This was always his dream—and it always seemed unattainable.

I was doing well in business, as were all my brothers. We had offered to buy him a truck, but he refused, saying, "If I don't buy it, I won't feel like it's mine."

Later that afternoon, when Dad stepped out of the doctor's office, his face was pale and gray. "Let's go," was all he said.

We rode in silence. I took the long way back to the station. We drove by our old house, the ball field, lake, and corner store, and Dad started talking about the memories each place held.

That's when I knew he was dying.

He looked at me and nodded.

I understood.

We stopped at Cabot's Ice Cream and had a cone together for the first time in fifteen years. We really talked that day. He told me how proud he was of all of us, and that he wasn't afraid of dying. His fear was of being away from my mother. Never had one man been more in love with a woman than my dad.

He made me promise that I would never tell anyone of his impending death. I agreed, knowing it was the toughest secret I'd ever have to keep.

At the time, my wife and I were looking to buy a truck. I asked Dad if he would go with me to see what I could get for a trade-in.

As we entered the showroom and I started talking with the salesman, I spotted Dad looking at the most beautiful, fully loaded, chocolate-brown, metal-flake pickup truck I had ever seen. He ran his hand over it like a sculptor checking his work.

I suggested to Dad that we take the brown truck out for a ride. We pulled out onto Route 27, my father behind the wheel. He drove for ten minutes, saying how beautifully it rode.

When we got back, we took out a smaller blue truck, a better truck for commuting because of its lower gas consumption. We returned and completed the deal with the salesman.

A few nights later, I asked Dad if he would come with me to pick up the truck. I think he agreed so quickly just to get one final look at "my brown truck," as he called it.

When we pulled into the dealer's yard, there was my little blue truck with a SOLD sticker on it. Next to it was the brown pickup, all washed and shiny, with a big SOLD sign on the window.

I glanced at my father and saw the disappointment register on his face as he said, "Someone bought themselves a beautiful truck."

I just nodded and said, "Dad, would you go inside and tell the salesman I'll be right in as soon as I park the car?" As my father walked past the brown truck, he ran his hand along it and I could see the look of disappointment pass over his face again.

I pulled my car around to the far side of the building and looked through the showroom window at the man who had given up everything for his family. I watched as the salesman sat him down, handed him a set of keys to "his truck"—the brown one—and explained that it was for him from me, and this was our secret.

My dad looked out the window, our eyes met, and we both nodded and laughed.

I was waiting outside my house when my dad pulled up that night. As he stepped out of "his truck," I gave him a big hug and a kiss and told him how much I loved him, and reminded him this was our secret.

We went for a drive that evening. Dad said he understood the truck, but what was the significance of the Coca-Cola bottle cap with the star in the center taped to the steering wheel?

MY FATHER'S ARMS

H. MICHAEL BREWER

'VE NEVER SEEN GOD'S arms, but I know what they are like because I remember my father's arms.

My father was a carpenter, his skin burned coffee brown to the edge of his T-shirt sleeves. My father had the skilled arms of a craftsman, and he moved with quiet confidence. From watching my father, I learned the value of a day's work, the beauty of the finishing touch, the joy of accomplishment.

I remember my father's arms, sheened with sweat, salted with sawdust, trembling with fatigue when long hours would scarcely keep food on the table. In later years my father's wrists swelled with arthritis, the legacy of swinging a hammer and

pushing the heavy rotary saw, and the cost of providing for his family.

I remember my father's arms, muscled and powerful, strong enough to hoist a son into the air and settle him on sky-high shoulders. My father taught me to pass a football, cast a line, drive a nail. His arms were strong enough to be gentle, to hug the tears away, to hold the world at bay.

I remember my father's arms on the day my dog fell into a deep posthole at a construction site. Lying on the ground, cheek pressed into the rough dirt, my father reached into the hole, strained until his fingertips snagged the dog's collar, and brought him back into the light. That day I believed my father could do anything and nothing was beyond his reach.

I remember my father's arms, scarred by flying nails, jagged wood, and rough work, the mementos of doing what must be done without complaints or excuses. My small fingers used to trace the calluses on his palms, and I learned that nothing worthwhile comes without effort. Even love is sometimes built on toil and blood.

I remember my father's arms side by side with my own. I held the plywood in place while he nailed. Staring straight at the work, he said, "I love you, and I'm proud of you." Our eyes didn't meet. There was no need. I squeezed his shoulder, and we both understood.

Much of what I know about God I learned from my father, from his arms, his deeds, his touch. Jesus' father was a carpenter too, and as a child Jesus must have learned about God from watching Joseph. No wonder many years later Jesus taught His disciples to think of God as a heavenly Father.

I've never seen God's arms, but I know what they are like because I remember my father's arms.

SIMPLE WOODEN BOXES

MARTHA PENDERGRASS TEMPLETON

I SUPPOSE EVERYONE has a particular childhood Christmas that stands out more than any other. For me, it was the year that the Burlington factory in Scottsboro closed down. I was only a small child. I could not name for you the precise year; it is an insignificant blur in my mind, but the events of that Christmas will live forever in my heart.

My father, who had been employed at Burlington, never let on to us that we were having financial difficulties. After all, children live in a naïve world in which money and jobs are nothing more than jabberwocky, and for us the excitement of Christmas could never be squelched. We knew only that our daddy, who usually worked long, difficult hours, was now home more than we had ever remembered; each day seemed to be a holiday.

Mama, a homemaker, now sought work in the local textile mills, but jobs were scarce. Time after time, she was told no openings were available before Christmas, and it was on the way home from one such distressing interview that she wrecked our only car. Daddy's meager unemployment check would now be our family's only source of income. For my parents, the Christmas season brought mounds of worries, crowds of sighs, and tears and cascades of prayers.

I can only imagine what transpired between my parents in those moments when the answer came. Perhaps it took a while for the ideas to fully form.

Perhaps it was a merging of ideas from both of my parents. I don't know for sure how the idea took life, but somehow it did. They would scrape together enough money to buy each of us a Barbie doll. For the rest of our presents, they would rely on their talents, using scraps of materials they already had.

While dark, calloused hands sawed, hammered, and painted, nimble fingers fed dress after dress into the sewing machine. Barbie-sized bridal gowns, evening gowns…miniature clothes for every imaginable occasion pushed forward from the rattling old machine. Where we were while all this was taking place, I have no idea. But somehow my parents found time to pour themselves into our gifts, and the excitement of Christmas was once again born for the entire family.

That Christmas Eve, the sun was just setting over the distant horizon when I heard the roar of an unexpected motor in the driveway. Looking outside, I could hardly believe my eyes. Uncle Buck and Aunt Charlene, Mama's sister and her husband, had driven all the way from Georgia to surprise us. Packed tightly in their car, as though no air were needed, sat my three cousins, my Aunt Dean, who refused to be called "Aunt," and both

my grandparents. I also couldn't help but notice innumerable gifts for all of us, all neatly packaged and tied with beautiful bows. They had known that it would be a difficult Christmas and they had come to help.

The next morning we awoke to more gifts than I ever could have imagined. And, though I don't have one specific memory of what any of the toys were, I know that there were mountains of toys. Toys! Toys! Toys!

And it was there, amidst all that jubilation, that Daddy decided not to give us his gifts. With all the toys we had gotten, there was no reason to give us the dollhouses that he had made. They were rustic and simple red boxes, after all. Certainly not as good as the store-bought gifts that Mama's family had brought. The music of laughter filled the morning, and we never suspected that, hidden somewhere, we each had another gift.

When Mama asked Daddy about the gifts, he confided his feelings, but she insisted he give us our gifts. And so, late that afternoon, after all of the guests had gone, Daddy reluctantly brought his gifts of love to the living room.

Wooden boxes. Wooden boxes, painted red, with hinged lids, so that each side could be opened and used as a house. On either side was a compartment just big enough to store a Barbie doll, and all the way across, a rack on which to hang our Barbie clothes. On the outside was a handle, so that when it was closed, held by a magnet that looked remarkably like an equal sign, the house could be carried suitcase style. And, though I don't really remember any of the other gifts I got that day, those boxes are indelibly etched into my mind. I remember the texture of the wood, the exact shade of red paint, the way the pull of the magnet felt when I closed the lid, the time-darkened handles and hinges…I remember how the clothes hung delicately on the hangers inside, and how I had to be careful not to pull Barbie's hair when I closed the lid. I remember everything that is possibly rememberable, because we kept and cherished those boxes long after our Barbie doll days were over.

I have lived and loved twenty-nine Christmases, each new and fresh with an air of excitement all its own. Each filled with love and hope. Each bringing gifts, cherished and longed for. But few of those gifts compare with those simple wooden boxes. So it is no wonder that I get teary-eyed when I think of my father, standing there on that cold Christmas morning, wondering if his gift was good enough.

Love, Daddy, is always good enough.

*I*n previous generations, fathers were nearly always the exclusive family breadwinner. Today, however, it is a fact of life that the majority of mothers work outside the home. I understand the financial constraints that make it necessary for many of them, but I do regret it. The obvious reason is that children lose time and attention they might otherwise receive from their working mothers. Yet fathers lose something too.

Historically, men have understood intuitively that they are expected to provide for their wives and children. It is one of the contributions for which men are designed, physically and emotionally. They take great satisfaction in what they contribute, materially and otherwise, to the welfare of their families. It is this masculine identity that links a man to his wife and children and gives him a sense of pride and accomplishment in his manhood. If taken away, his commitment to his family is jeopardized.

Let me personalize the concept. Within a lifetime of responsibilities and professional assignments, I have drawn the greatest satisfaction from the fact that I have cared for each member of my family for more than thirty years. I have worked hard to provide the necessities and a few luxuries for them. I have dedicated myself to their welfare. My identity is inextricably linked with that family commitment. If my role as provider had been taken away from me, much of the joy in family life would have gone with it.

Sociologists tell us that unmarried young men are at risk for many antisocial behaviors. But when a man falls in love with a woman, dedicating himself to care for her and protect her and support her, he becomes the mainstay of social order. Instead of using his energies to pursue his own lusts and desires, he sweats to build a home and save for the future and seek the best job available. His selfish impulses are inhibited. His sexual passions are channeled. He discovers a sense of pride—yes, masculine pride—because he is needed by his wife and children. Suddenly we see the beauty of the divine plan.

Jesus tells us in Scripture that fathers understand how to and clearly desire to give "good gifts" to their children (Matthew 7:9–11). For a dad, providing for one's family is more than a duty—it is an expression of love, and one of the most fulfilling assignments he will ever undertake.

Even more important, it is exactly as almighty God, the Father of all fathers, intended.

James Dobson

A FATHER,
A SPIRITUAL ROLE MODEL

"Bring (your children) up in the *training* and instruction of the *Lord*."

EPHESIANS 6:4

YOU CANNOT OUTGIVE GOD

DR. JAMES DOBSON

I LEARNED TO GIVE A tenth of my income to the church when I was a preschool lad. My grandmother would give me a dollar every now and then, and she always instructed me to place a dime of it in the church offering the next Sunday morning. I have tithed from that day to this. I also watched my father give of his limited resources, not only to the church, but to anyone in need.

My dad was the original soft touch to those who were hungry. He was an evangelist who journeyed from place to place to hold revival meetings. Travel was expensive, and we never seemed to have much more money than was absolutely necessary. One of the problems was the way churches paid their ministers in those days. Pastors received a year-round salary, but evangelists were paid only when they

worked. Therefore, my father's income stopped abruptly during Thanksgiving, Christmas, summer vacation, or any time he rested. Perhaps that's why we were always near the bottom of the barrel when he was at home. But that didn't stop my father from giving.

I remember Dad going off to speak in a tiny church and coming home ten days later. My mother greeted him warmly and asked how the revival had gone. He was always excited about that subject. Eventually, in moments like this she would get around to asking him about the offering. Women have a way of worrying about things like that.

"How much did they pay you?" she asked.

I can still see my father's face as he smiled and looked at the floor. "Aw...," he stammered. My mother stepped back and looked into his eyes.

"Oh, I get it," she said. "You gave the money away again, didn't you?"

"Myrt," he said. "The pastor there is going through a hard time. His kids are so needy. It just broke my heart. They have holes in their shoes, and one of them is going to school on these cold mornings without a coat. I felt I should give the entire fifty dollars to them."

My good mother looked intently at him for a moment and then she smiled. "You know, if God told you to do it, it's okay with me."

Then a few days later the inevitable happened. The Dobsons ran completely out of money. There was no reserve to tide us over. That's when my father gathered us in the bedroom for a time of prayer. I remember that day as though it were yesterday. He prayed first.

"Oh, Lord, You promised that if we would be faithful with You and Your people in our good times, then You would not forget us in our time of need. We have tried to be generous with what You have given us, and now we are calling on You for help."

A very impressionable ten-year-old boy named Jimmy was watching and listening very carefully that day. *What will happen?* he wondered. *Did God hear Dad's prayer?*

The next day an unexpected check for $1,200 came for us in the mail. Honestly! That's the way it happened, not just this once but many times. I saw the Lord match my dad's giving stride for stride. No, God never made us wealthy, but my young faith grew by leaps and bounds. I learned that you *cannot* outgive God!

My father continued to give generously through the midlife years and into his sixties. I used to worry about how he and Mom would fund their retirement years because they were able to save very little money. If Dad did get many dollars ahead, he'd give them away. I wondered how in the world they would live on the pittance paid to retired ministers by our denomination.

One day my father was lying on the bed, and Mom was getting dressed. She turned to look at him and he was crying.

"What's the matter?" she asked.

"The Lord just spoke to me," he replied.

"Do you want to tell me about it?" she prodded.

"He told me something about you," Dad said.

She then demanded that he tell her what the Lord had communicated to him.

My father said, "It was a strange experience. I was just lying there thinking about many things. I wasn't praying or even thinking about you when the Lord spoke to me and said, 'I'm going to take care of Myrtle.'"

Neither of them understood the message, but simply filed it away in the catalog of imponderables. But five days later my dad had a massive heart attack, and three months after that he was gone. At sixty-six years of age, this good man whose name I share went out to meet the Christ whom he had loved and served all those years.

It was thrilling to witness the way God fulfilled His promise to take care of my mother. Even when she was suffering from end-stage Parkinson's disease and required constant care at an

astronomical cost, God provided. The small inheritance that Dad left to his wife multiplied in the years after his departure. It was sufficient to pay for everything she needed, including marvelous and loving care. God was with her in every other way, too, tenderly cradling her in His secure arms until He took her home.

In the end, my dad never came close to outgiving God.

I WAS ON HIS MIND

MICHAEL J. MASSIE

REMEMBER THE MAROON carpet that covered the basement steps in my parents' house on Andrew Avenue. My father used to spend countless hours with my sister and me playing on that carpet. A great deal of our playtime was in the basement or on those stairs. We would shoot down plastic cowboys and Indians with rubber bands, wrestle, and play hide-and-seek. I struggle now to remember the actual dimensions of our basement, but I will never forget the carpet, because it was on that carpet that my father demonstrated how much he loved his children by spending hours with us.

On December 28, 1981, my sister and I were in the basement playing with our new Christmas toys when we heard a thud from upstairs. Something was going on in the kitchen above our heads. I sensed that something was not quite right.

Normally, large thuds came from my sister and me knocking each other over. Usually our roughhousing was followed by choruses of blaming each other, and then one of us would spend some time in our room as punishment.

After a few minutes of silence from upstairs, my mother opened the basement door and called in a strained voice, "Mike, Devon, come up here for a minute."

"Why, Mom?" we replied in our typical childhood manner.

"Your dad wants to see you," she answered.

My sister and I raced to the top of the steps, but as we clambered through the basement doorway we were greeted by an unusual sight. Our father was lying on his back, staring blankly at the ceiling.

Dad reached out in our direction with one arm. "Come here and let me give you both a hug."

I had never seen my father in such a helpless position. His left arm lay next to his side, while he blindly gestured with his right arm for us to come to him. His words were calming, but nothing could keep down the panic that rose within my stomach as tears leapt to my eyes. Underneath his calm words was the pain of uncertainty. He

hugged my sister and me individually with one arm, not with the strength of his usual bear hugs.

His voice shook as he told us, "Everything will be okay. Listen to and obey your mother. I am going away for a while."

Without any further explanation my mother shuffled us back into the basement, and the door was closed solidly behind us. We were supposed to go back into the basement and resume playing. I'm sure my mother and father thought they were protecting us from some emotional harm, but neither one of us made it back down the steps. Instead, we sat by the door, huddled together with our faces on the maroon carpet, watching everything we could see through the crack at the bottom of the door.

It was the first time my sister and I actually sat quietly together without causing a fuss. Something serious was taking place. The thought of our father as blind, crippled, and maybe dying scared us. The only comfort we had was in each other and the familiar maroon carpet, which had been the playground upon which our father launched countless adventures.

As the lights from the ambulance reflected off the eggshell white walls, the feet of the EMTs walked past to check on our motionless father. As they wheeled in the stretcher, their muffled words penetrated the basement door. "Call ahead to the hospital…."

We watched and we waited. I had no answers for my younger sister's questions. When all was quiet, we retreated down the steps. After a short time my mother came downstairs and held us as we all cried. Fear and pain wracked my mother's voice as she explained, "Your father is very sick, and he had to go to the hospital, but he will be all right."

Several days later my sister and I were allowed to visit my father at the hospital. He grinned as we walked into the room. He was regaining some strength, but he was going to be in the hospital for quite some time. Through the next several weeks friends and relatives visited to lend their support, but the important part is that eventually Dad came home.

Over the years I have pieced together bits of information about what really happened that night. My father suffered from what doctors would later call a stroke. Dad refers to it as the day his "brain blew up." My father not only recovered, but his only side effect was the loss of a quarter of his eyesight. The blindness in the upper left-hand corners of his eyes is his constant reminder that he must rely on God to see things clearly. Dad memorized 1 Corinthians 13:12 to help him remember God's strength: "Now we see but a poor reflection as in a mirror; then we shall see face to face."

After the stroke, my father traveled to several churches in our hometown to give his testimony—his biggest audiences were church youth groups. On one occasion, when I was around the age of thirteen, I had the opportunity to go with my father and listen to his message. Until then I believed I'd heard all about how God had healed and continued to heal my father, but there was a part of his testimony that I had never heard before. It was a part that would change me spiritually—a part that would help me understand what it meant for God to love me unconditionally.

"As I lay on the floor, completely blind and not able to feel half of my body, I told my wife I wanted to see my children one last time. I was sure I was dying, but the irony was that even if my children had been right next to me, I wouldn't have been able to see them. My wife called Mike and Devon upstairs, and I placed my good arm around each of them in turn and told

them I loved them. I told them not to worry, that everything would be okay. Then I sent them back downstairs, not wanting to worry them. The ambulance arrived, and I was loaded into the back.

"At this point everyone wonders what you would say to God. Do you pray for the pain to stop? Do you pray for a quick death so that you can be

with the Lord? Do you pray to be healed instantly? I found myself praying the one thing that came to mind: 'Lord, when I die, don't let my children be bitter.' The most important thing for me at the time when I thought I was dying was that my children not grow to hate the God I loved so much."

My father continued to give the rest of his testimony, but I could hear nothing else. I now knew that my father's *last* thoughts as they were taking him away were of my little sister and me. I began to weep as I fully realized how unworthy I was of so great a love. I did nothing to deserve my father's love, and yet he gave it so freely that he was thinking of me while he thought he was dying.

When they put my dad into the back of that ambulance, he exhibited the unconditional love of God the Almighty. His only concern was for his children, no matter the pain, the suffering, and the proximity of death. Every time I see my father, I am reminded in some way of the unconditional love and grace that my heavenly Father has given to me.

No matter what the cost, I know that God loves me. I know this because my dad showed me what unconditional love is all about.

A SINGLE CROCUS

JOAN WESTER ANDERSON

T WAS AN AUTUMN morning shortly after my husband and I moved into our first house. Our children were upstairs unpacking, and I was looking out the window at my father moving around mysteriously on the front lawn. My parents lived nearby, and Dad had visited us several times already. "What are you doing out there?" I called to him.

He looked up, smiling. "I'm making you a surprise." Knowing my father, I thought it could be just about anything. A self-employed jobber, he was always building things out of odds and ends. When we were kids, he once rigged up a jungle gym out of wheels and pulleys. For one of my Halloween parties, he created an electrical pumpkin and mounted it on a broomstick. As guests came to our door, he would light the pumpkin and have it pop out in front of them from a hiding place in the bushes.

Today, however, Dad would say no more, and caught up in the busyness of our new life, I eventually forgot about his surprise.

Until one raw day the following March when I glanced out the window. Dismal. Overcast. Little piles of dirty snow still stubbornly littering the lawn. Would winter ever end?

And yet…was it a mirage? I strained to see what I thought was something pink, miraculously peeking out of a drift. And was that a dot of blue across the yard, a small note of optimism in this gloomy expanse? I grabbed my coat and headed outside for a closer look.

They were crocuses, scattered whimsically throughout the front lawn. Lavender, blue, yellow, and my favorite pink—little faces bobbing in the bitter wind.

Dad, I smiled, remembering the bulbs he had secretly planted last fall. He knew how the darkness and dreariness of winter always got me

down. What could have been more perfectly timed, more attuned to my needs? How blessed I was, not only for the flowers but for him.

My father's crocuses bloomed each spring for the next four or five seasons, bringing that same assurance every time they arrived: *Hard times almost over. Hold on, keep going, light is coming soon.*

Then a spring came with only half the usual blooms. The next spring there were none. I missed the crocuses, but my life was busier than ever, and I had never been much of a gardener. I would ask Dad

to come over and plant new bulbs. But I never did.

He died suddenly one October day. My family grieved deeply, leaning on our faith. I missed him terribly, though I knew he would always be a part of us.

Four years passed, and on a dismal spring afternoon I was running errands and found myself feeling depressed. *You've got the winter blahs again,* I told myself. You get them every year; it's chemistry. But it was something else too.

It was Dad's birthday, and I found myself thinking about him. This was not unusual—my family often talked about him, remembering how he lived his faith. Once I saw him take off his coat and give it to a homeless man. Often he'd chat with strangers passing by his storefront, and if he learned they were poor and hungry, he would invite them home for a meal. But now, in the car, I couldn't help wondering, *How* is he now? *Where* is he? Is there really a heaven?

I felt guilty for having doubts, but sometimes, I thought as I turned into our driveway, faith is so hard.

Suddenly I slowed, stopped, and stared at the lawn. Muddy grass and small gray mounds of melting snow. And there, bravely waving in the wind, was one pink crocus.

How could a flower bloom from a bulb more than eighteen years old, one that had not blossomed in over a decade? But there was the crocus. Tears filled my eyes as I realized its significance.

Hold on, keep going, light is coming soon. The pink crocus bloomed for only a day. But it built my faith for a lifetime.

I will always be grateful that throughout his life my father demonstrated an unshakable commitment to the Lord. James Dobson Sr. was a man of many intense loves, but his greatest passion was expressed in his love for Jesus Christ. His every thought and deed were motivated or influenced by his desire to serve his Lord. I can truthfully say that we were never together without my being drawn closer to God by being in his presence.

We have already talked about many critical responsibilities of fatherhood, yet none rank higher in significance than the task of leading your children to Christ. Dads, you simply must *provide* spiritual direction at home. This is accomplished when you read the Scriptures to your children, teach them the fundamentals of their faith, explain your family's moral values and sacred traditions, and make sure that your children worship regularly in church. Perhaps most important of all, you must model a life that demonstrates love for God on a daily basis.

Believe it or not, my parents introduced me to Jesus Christ when I was only three years of age. I remember the occasion clearly. I was attending a Sunday evening church service and was sitting near the back with my mother. My father was the pastor who invited those who wished to do so to come forward. Without asking my mother, I stepped out into the aisle and knelt at a wooden alter. I recall crying and asking Jesus to forgive my sins. It is over-whelming for me now to imagine the King of the universe caring about an insignificant kid barely out of toddlerhood!

Not all children will heed a call to faith that early or dramat-ically, of course—nor should they be expected to. Yet it is important to note that my own conversion at that young age was possible because of my parents' example. From my first days, I saw them on their knees, praying and talking to the Lord. They later told me that I attempted to pray before I learned to talk, imitating the sounds I had heard.

If you set a faithful example beginning with the day your sons and daughters are born, they will never forget what they have seen and heard. As parents, this is our privilege and duty as outlined in Scripture: "Bring [your children] up in the training and instruction of the Lord" (Ephesians 6:4).

My dad, along with my mother, succeeded in this task while raising me, and though I occasionally fell short of the standard, I did my very best to achieve the same at home with my children. Shirley and I continue to give thanks to God that Danae and Ryan *are not only believers, but are also actively serving the Lord in many ways.*

The vital mission of introducing your children to the Christian faith can be likened to a relay race. First, your parents run their lap around the track, carrying the baton, which represents the gospel of Jesus Christ. At the appropriate moment, they hand the baton to you, and you begin your journey around the track. Finally, the time comes when you must get the baton safely into the hands of your child. But as any track coach will testify, relay races are won or lost in the transfer of the baton. *This is the critical moment when all can be ruined by a fumble or miscalculation. Any failure is most likely to occur in this exchange. Once firmly gripped, however, the baton is rarely dropped on the backstretch of the track.*

As fathers, our most important reason for living is to get the baton—the gospel—safely into the hands of our children (John 3:3). More than anything else that you will achieve in your earthly years, it is success in this single endeavor that will qualify you for the title of "hero." All else pales in comparison.

And when your sons and daughters cross the finish line of life with their commitment to Jesus Christ intact, they—and you—will bask in the applause of heaven.

James Dobson

ACKNOWLEDGMENTS

"Standing Tall" by Steve Farrar. From *Standing Tall* by Steve Farrar
(Sisters, Ore.: Multnomah Publishers, Inc., 1994).
Used by permission of Multnomah Publishers, Inc.

"Head of the House" by Thom Hunter. From *Those Not-So-Still Small Voices*
(Colorado Springs, Colo.: NavPress, 1993).
Used by permission of the author.

"Just Waitin' for You" by Stu Weber. From *Four Pillars of a Man's Heart*
by Stu Weber (Sisters, Ore.: Multnomah Publishers, Inc., 1997).
Used by permission of Multnomah Publishers, Inc.

"Of More Value" by Jerry B. Jenkins. From *Still the One* by Jerry B. Jenkins
(Colorado Springs, Colo.: Focus on the Family, 1995).
Used by permission of the author.

"Manhood at Its Best" by Dr. James Dobson. From *Stories of the Heart & Home*
(Sisters, Ore.: Multnomah Publishers, Inc., 2000).
Used by permission of Multnomah Publishers, Inc.

"A Secret Promise Kept" by Brian Keefe. © 1993.
Used by permission of the author.

"My Father's Arms" by H. Michael Brewer. © 2001.
Used by permission of the author.

"Simple Wooden Boxes" by Martha Pendergrass Templeton. © 1995.
Used by permission of the author.

"You Cannot Outgive God" by Dr. James Dobson. From *Stories of
the Heart & Home* (Sisters, Ore.: Multnomah Publishers, Inc., 2000).
Used by permission of Multnomah Publishers, Inc.

"I Was on His Mind" by Michael J. Massie. © 2001.
Used by permission of the author. Michael Massie writes, "Many thanks to
Wayne Holmes and his book, *The Heart of a Father*."

"A Single Crocus" by Joan Wester Anderson. From *Where Wonders Prevail*
by Joan Wester Anderson © 1996 by Joan Wester Anderson.
Used by permission of Ballantine books, a division of Random House, Inc.

ART INDEX

The *heart* of every child
beats to the *rhythm*
of a *father's* love.

STEVEN R. CURLEY